OBISPO y MONSERRATE
LA HABANA · CUBA

ISBN 978-1-61427-934-1

Martino Publishing
Mansfield Centre, CT
2016

COCKTAILS

ABC COCKTAIL

½ Port Wine.
½ Fine Cognac.
1/3 Marraschino.
1 Dash Angostura.
Several sprigs Peppermint.
Peel of a lemon.
½ Teaspoonful of Sugar.
Plenty ice in a glass of 6 ounce.

Shake a little and serve with two cherries.

½ Vino de Oporto.
½ Cognac fino.
1/3 Marrasquino.
1 Gota Angostura.
Varias ramas de hierba buena.
La corteza de un limón.
½ Cucharadita de azúcar.
Hielo abundante en un vaso de 6 onzas. Bátase ligeramente y sírvase sin colar con 2 guindas verdes.

ABSINTHE DROP

En una copa de 10 onzas.

¼ Anisette.

2 Onzas Absinthe Pernot.

Hielo menudo en el colador. Agua natural hasta llenarla.

Use a 10-ounce glass.

¼ Anisette.

2 Ounces Pernot Absinthe

Cracked ice in the strainer.

Fill glass to the brim with natural water.

APERITAL COCKTAIL

2 Onzas Aperital Delor.
La piel de un limón verde.
1 Cucharadita Granadina.
Hielo abundante.
Batido y sírvase sin colar.

2 Ounces Aperital Delor.
The peel on an unripe lemon
1 Teaspoonful Grenadine.
Cracked Ice.
Shake well and serve without straining.

ALEXANDER

1/3 Crema fresca leche.
1/3 Gin Gordon.
1/3 Crema Cacao.
1 Cucharadita de azúcar.
La piel entera de un limón.
Hielo menudo. Muy batido y colado.

1/3 Fresh Sweet Cream.
1/3 Gordon Gin.
1/3 Creme de Cacao.
1 Teaspoonful Sugar.
1 Full Lemon Peel.
Plenty of cracked ice.
Shake well and strain into cocktail glass.

BLIND GEN

2 Yemas de huevos sin clara en una copa de Vino Moscatel o Vermouth Martini Rossi.

The Yolks of 2 Eggs.

1 Glass Moscatel Wine or Martini Rossi Vermouth.

BUTTERFLY
(Absinthe Frappe)

En una copa de 10 onzas con hielo menudo y abundante.

Agua azucarada hasta casi llenarla.
2 Onzas Absinthe Pernot flotando. Disuélvase lentamente con una cucharita hasta que se quede muy bien ligado.

Use a 10-ounce glass.

Plenty of cracked ice.

Fill glass almost to the brim with sweetened water.

2 Ounces Pernot Absinthe.

Stir slowly with a spoon until well mixed; then drink

BRANDY COCKTAIL

En un vaso de 10 onzas.
Hielo menudo.
Una ramita hierba buena.
La cáscara de un limón verde con el jugo exprimido dentro.
½ Cucharadita de azúcar.
1 Gota Angostura.
½ Cucharadita Curacao.
2 Onzas Cognac Tres Copas.
Agítese de un vaso para el otro. Sírvase colado.

Use 10-ounce glass.
Cracked Ice.
1 Sprig of Mint.
1 Unripe Lemon Peel, squeezing juice in glass.
½ Teaspoonful Sugar.
1 Drop Angostura.
½ Teaspoonful Curacao.
2 Ounces Tres Copas cognac.
Shake lightly and strain; then, serve.

BRANDY FLIP

1 Copa Cognac Tres Copas.
1 Cucharada de azúcar.
1 Huevo entero.
Hielo abundante.
Muy batido y sírvase colado y adornado con canela en polvo.

1 Glass Tres Copas Cognac.
1 Spoonful Sugar.
1 Whole Egg.
Plenty cracked ice.
Shake well and strain; then, serve with powdered cinnamon on top.

BRANDY COCKTAIL

2 Brandy (2 onzas).
1 Gota de Angostura.
½ Cucharadita Curacao.
1 Ramita hierba buena.
Cáscara limón con su jugo.
½ Cucharadita de azúcar.
Batido y Colado.

2 Ounces Brandy.
1 Dash Angostura Bitters.
½ Teaspoonful Curacao.
1 Small Sprig of Mint.
½ Teaspoonful Sugar.
1 Lemon Peel.
Shake well and strain.

No es lo mismo tres copas de un Coñac, que un Coñac TRES COPAS

BRANDY DAISSY

una copa llena de hielo menudo.
1 Gota Angostura.
½ Cucharadita de Chatreusse amarillo.
2 Onzas Cognac Tres Copas.
½ Cáscara limón verde y jugo.
Unas ramitas hierba buena.
Dos guindas. Sírvase sin colar.

A glass full of cracked ice.
1 Dash Angostura.
½ Teaspoonful Yellow Chartreuse.
2 Ounces Tres Copas Cognac.
½ Lemon Peel
Several sprigs of Mint.
2 Cherries.
Stir and serve without straining.

BRONX

1|3 Vermouth Martini Rossi
1|3 Vermouth Nolly Prat.
1|3 Gin Gordon.
½ Cucharadita Curacao.
1 Cucahadita jugo naranja.
Hielo menudo. Ligeramente batido y colado.

1|3 Martini Rossi Vermouth
1|3 Nolly Prat Vermouth.
1|3 Gordon Gin.
½ Teaspoonful Curacao.
1 Teaspoonful Orange Juice.
Cracked Ice.
Shake lightly and strain; then, serve.

BRONX NUM. 2

1|3 Vermouth Martini Rossi
1|3 Vermouth Nolly Prat.
1|3 Gin Gordon
½ Cucharadita Curacao.
Hielo menudo. Enfríese sin batirlo y cuélese. Sírvase con una piel de naranja y dos guindas.

1|3 Martini Rossi Vermouth
1|3 Nolly Prat Vermouth.
1|3 Gordon Gin.
½ Teaspoonful Curacao.
Cracked Ice.
Do not shake. Strain and serve very cold with an orange peel and 2 cherries.

BLUE PARADISE

½ Dubonnet.
½ Cognac Tres Copas.
1/3 Perfait Amour.
La cáscara de un limón.
Hielo menudo. Batido y colado.

½ Dubonnet.
½ Tres Copas Cognac.
1/3 Perfait Amour.
1 Lemon Peel.
Cracked Ice.
Shake well and strain into cocktail glass.

BLUE MOON

½ Crema Violeta.
½ Cognac Tres Copas.
½ Cucharadita Menta verde.
Hielo abundante. Batido y colado.

½ Creme de Violete.
½ Tres Copas Cognac.
½ Teaspoonful Green Creme de Menthe.
Plenty of cracked ice.
Shake well and strain into a cocktail glass.

BETWEEN - SHEETS

1/3 Cognac Tres Copas.
1/3 Crema Cacao.
1/3 Crema de leche fresca.
1 Gota Angostura.
1 Cucharadita de azúcar.
La cáscara de un limón.
Hielo abundante. Muy batido.

1/3 Tres Copas Cognac.
1/3 Creme de Cacao.
1/3 Fresh Sweet Cream.
1 Dash Angostura.
1 Teaspoonful Sugar.
1 Lemon Peel.
Plenty of Cracked ice.
Shake well and strain into cocktail glass.

CORONEL BATISTA
(Especial)

½ Vermouth Torino.
½ Ron Carta Blanca.
Jugo de ½ limón.
½ Cucharadita de azúcar.
Bátase perfectamente con hielo menudo, cuélese y sírvase con una lasca de piña y dos guindas.

½ Torino Vermouth.
½ Carta Blanca Rum.
The juice of ½ lemon.
½ Teaspoonful of Sugar.
Shake well and strain with crushed ice serve with one slice of pineapple and two cherries.

CHAPARRA

½ Ron Martí.
½ Vermouth Martini Rossi.
La cáscara de un limón verde bien estrujada con el hielo.
½ Cucharadita azúcar.
Enfríese sin batirlo, y cuélese dejando el limón en forma espiral en la copa.

½ Martí Rum.
½ Martini Rossi Vermouth
½ Teaspoonful Sugar.
1 Lemon Peel thoroughly squeezed.
Do not shake. Strain and serve very cold leaving lemon peel in glass in the shape of a spiral.

CAFFERY SPECIAL COCKTAIL

2 Oz. Sloe Gin.
1 Cucharadita de jugo de naranja.
1 Cucharadita de Apricot Brandy.
½ Cucharadita de jarabe Granadina.
Hielo abundante. En una copa de forma cónica de 6 onzas, adornado con lascas de piña y dos guindas.

2 Oz. Sloe Gin.
1 Teaspoonful orange juice.
1 Teaspoonful Apricot Brandy.
½ Teaspoonful Grenadine Sirup.
Plenty Ice.
In a cognac glass of 6 Oz.
Serve with slices of pinapple and two cherries.

CALEDONIA
(Special)

1/3 Crema Cacao.
1/3 Cognac Tres Copas.
1/3 Leche fresca.
1 Gota Angostura.
1 Yema de huevo.
La Cáscara de un limón.
Hielo menudo. Batido y colado. Adórnese con canela.

1/3 Creme de Cacao.
1/3 Tres Copas Cognac.
1/3 Fresh sweet milk.
The Yolk of 1 Egg.
1 Dash Angostura.
1 Lemon Peel.
Crushed Ice.
Shake well and strain. Serve in cocktail glass with Cinnamon on top.

CLEOPATRA

½ Vino Oporto.
½ Cognac Tres Copas
1/3 Cointreau.
1/3 Jugo de piña.
Hielo menudo. Batido v colado.

½ Port Wine.
½ Tres Copas Cognac.
1/3 Cointreau.
1/3 Pineapple Juice.
Cracked Ice.
Shake well and strain into cocktail glass.

CASIANO COCKTAIL

2 Onzas de Vermouth Martini Rossi.
1 Cucharada Crema Cassis.
La piel de un limón.
Hielo menudo.
Batido y colado.

2 Ounces Martini Rossi Vermouth.
1 Teaspoonful Creme Cassis
1 Lemon Peel.
Cracked Ice.
Shake and strain then, serve.

CAFE COCKTAIL

1 Café puro.
½ Crema Cacao.
½ Cognac Soberano.
1 Cucharadita azúcar.
La cáscara de un limón.
Hielo menudo. Batido y colado.

1 Black Coffee.
½ Creme de Cacao.
½ Soberano Cognac.
1 Teaspoonful Sugar.
1 Lemon Peel.
Cracked Ice.
Shake well and strain into cocktail glass.

CLOVER CLUB

2 Onzas Gin Gordon.
Varias gotas Menta blanca.
El jugo de ½ limón verde.
1 Cucharadita Granadina.
La clara de un huevo.
Hielo menudo. Bien batido y colado.

2 Ounces Gordon Gin.
Several Dashes White Mint.
The juice of ½ Lemon.
1 Teaspoonful Grenadine.
Plenty of Cracked Ice.
The White of 1 Egg.
Shake well and strain into cocktail glass.

CHAPARRON

2/3 Cognac Tres Copas.
1/3 Vermouth Martini Rossi
La cáscara de un limón completo en espiral en la copa.
½ Cucharadita de azúcar.
Bien mojada la piel del limón con el azúcar para que quede bien saturada de su perfume. Enfríese y cuélese. Sírvase con la piel dentro de la copa.

2/3 Tres Copas Cognac.
1/3 Martini Rossi Vermouth
1 Lemon Peel forming a spiral.
½ Teaspoonful Sugar.
Mix thoroughly lemon peel with sugar so as to saturate the concoction with the extract of the lemon. Strain and serve very cold with the lemon peel inside of glass.

CHAMPAGNE PUNCH
(100 Glasses)

2½ Libras azúcar.
2 Onzas Angostura.
1 Nuez Moscada y molida.
1 Piña blanca cortada menudita.
4 Melocotones cortados menuditos.
½ Pomo de guindas.
Corteza de dos limones.
Corteza de dos naranjas.
1 Botella Crema de Cacao.
1 Botella Apricot Brandy.
1 Botella de Cognac fino.
6 Botellas de Champagne.
6 Botellas de vino blanco.
(En una heladera, con hielo y sal granizada exteriormente).

2½ Pound of sugar.
2 Oz. Angostura.
1 Grated nutmes.
1 White pineapple small slices.
4 Peaches cut into small pieces.
½ Bottle of Cherries.
Peel of 2 lemons.
Peel of 2 oranges.
1 Bottle Creme de Cacao.
1 Bottle Apricot Brandy.
1 Bottle Fine Cognac.
6 Bottles Champagne.
6 Bottles White Wine.
(In one Punch - bowl with ice and salt outward)

CHAMPAGNE COCKTAIL

En una copa flouriforme de 10 onzas, llena de hielo menudo, póngase:
1 Terrón de azúcar.
1 Ramita hierba buena.
La piel de un limón.
Llénese con Champagne y adórnese con guindas.

In a 10-ounce glass filled with cracked ice, add.
1 Lump of sugar.
1 Sprig of mint.
1 Lemon peel.
Fill the glass to the brim with Champagne and garnish with cherries.

— **De "Tres Copas" una copa antes de tomar la sopa** —

CHANTECLAIR

½ Cognac Soberano.
½ Vermouth Ama.
1 Cucharadita Curacao.
Enfríese y cuélese sin batir. Sírvase y cuélese con dos guindas.

½ Soberano Cognac.
½ Ama Vermouth.
1 Teaspoonful Curacao.
Do not shake. Strain and served iced with 2 cherries.

CHIC

¼ Jugo Toronja.
½ Vermouth Martini Rossi.
½ Sloe Gin Gordon.
1 Cucharadita Marraschino
Hielo menudo. Muy batido y colado. Sírvase con varias almendras.

¼ Grape Fruit.
½ Martini Rossi Vermouth
½ Gordon's Sloe Gin.
1 Teaspoonful Marraschino
Cracked Ice.
Shake very well and strain into cocktail glass. Serve with a few almonds.

DAIQUIRI NUM. 1

2 Onzas Ron "Martí".
1 Cucharadita de azúcar.
El jugo de ½ limón verde.
Hielo menudito.
Bátase perfectamente y cuélese.

2 Ounces "Martí" Rum.
1 Teaspoonful Sugar.
Juice of ½ Lemon.
Cracked Ice.
Shake well and strain into cocktail glass.

DAIQUIRI NUM. 2

2 Onzas Ron "Martí".
Unas gotas de Curacao.
1 Cucharadita jugo naranja.
1 Cucharadita de azúcar.
El jugo de ½ limón verde.
Hielo menudito.
Batido y colado.

2 Ounces "Martí" Rum.
Several Dashes Curacao.
1 Teaspoonful Orange Juice.
1 Teaspoonful Sugar.
Juice of ½ Lemon.
Cracked Ice.
Shake well and strain into cocktail glass.

DAIQUIRI NUM. 3
(Benjamín Orbon)

2 Onzas Ron "Martí".
1 Cucharada de azúcar.
1 Cucharadita jugo de toronja.
1 Cucharadita Marraschino.
El jugo de ½ limón verde.
Hielo frappe.
Batido y sírvase frappe.

2 Ounces "Martí" Rum.
1 Spoonful Sugar.
1 Teaspoonful Grape Fruit Juice.
1 Teaspoonful Marrasquino.
Juice of ½ Lemon.
Shake well and strain into cocktail glass. Serve frappe.

DAIQUIRI NUM 4
(Florida Style)

2 Onzas Ron "Martí".
1 Cucharadita de azúcar.
1 Cucharadita Marraschino.
El jugo de ½ limón verde.
Batido eléctricamente con heilo pulverizado. Sírvase frappe.

2 Ounces "Martí" Rum.
1 Spoonful Sugar.
1 Teaspoonful Marrasquino.
Juice of ½ Lemon.
Shake with cracked ice.
Serve frappe.

DIAMOND HITCH

En un vaso de 12 onzas.
2 Onzas Ginebra.
1 Gota Angostura.
Piel de un limón.
Hielo menudo.
Champagne hasta llenarlo sin colar.

Use a 10-ounce glass.
2 Ounces Gin.
1 Dash Angostura.
1 Lemon Peel.
Plenty Cracked Ice.
Fill glass to the brim with Champagne.
Do not strain.

DELIO NUÑEZ

1/3 Jugo Toronja.
½ Gin Gordon.
½ Cucharadita azúcar.
1 Cucharadita Marraschino
½ Clara de huevo.
Hielo menudo. Muy batido y colado.

1/3 Grape Fruit Juice.
½ Gordon Gin.
½ Teaspoonful Sugar.
1 Teaspoonful Marrasquino
Shake well and strain into Half of the white of an egg cocktail glass.

EUREKA

½ Sloe Gin Gallo.
½ Calvados.
1 Cucharadita de jugo de limón.
1 Cucharadita Sherry Brandy.
Hielo menudo. Batido y colado.

½ Gordon's Sloe Gallo.
½ Calvados.
1 Teaspoonful Lemon Juice.
1 Teaspoonful Sherry Brandy.
Cracked Ice.
Shake well and strain into cocktail glass.

EGG-NOG

1 Cucharada de azúcar.
2 Onzas Cognac Tres Copas.
6 Onzas leche fresca.
Hielo batido y colado.
Adornado con canela en polvo. Uno o dos huevos adentro.

1 Spoonful Sugar.
2 Ounces Tres Copas Cognac.
2 Eggs.
Cracked Ice.
Shake well and strain; then, serve.

FORESTIER
(Special)

1/3 Crema Cacao.
1/3 Gin Gordon.
1/3 Leche fresca.
1/6 Cointreau
½ Cucharadita de azúcar.
Hielo abundante. Muy batido y colado.

1/3 Creme de Cacao.
1/3 Gordon Gin.
1/6 Cointreau.
½ Teaspoonful Sugar.
Plenty of Ice.
Shake well and strain; then serve.

FLORIDITA SPECIAL

1/3 Rye Whiskey.
½ Vermouth Martini Rossi.
1 Cucharadita Amer Picón.
½ Cucharadita Curacao.
½ Cucharadita azúcar.
1 Gota Angostura.
1 Cáscara pequeña limón.
Hielo menudo. Batido y colado.

1/3 Rye Whisky.
½ Martini Rossi Vermouth.
1 Teaspoonful Amer Picon
½ Teaspoonful Curacao.
½ Teaspoonful Sugar.
1 Dash Angostura.
1 Small Lemon Peel.
Cracked Ice.
Shake well and strain into cocktail glass.

GOLDEN DAWN

½ Calvados Apple Jack
½ Gin Gordon.
1/3 Apricot Brandy.
½ Cucharadita Granadina.
1 Cucharadita Jugo Naranja.

Hielo menudo. Batido y colado. Sírvase con una guinda

½ Calvados or Applejack.
½ Gordon Gin.
1/3 Apricot Brandy.
½ Teaspoonful Grenadine.
1 Teaspoonful Orange Juice.
Cracked Ice.
Shake well and strain. Serve in cocktail glass with one cherry.

GREEN FIZZ

2 Onzas Gin Gordon.
1 Cucharadita de azúcar.
1 Cucharadita Menta verde.
Jugo de ½ limón.
1 Clara de huevo.
Hielo menudo. Muy batido y colado.

2 Ounces Gordon Gin.
1 Teaspoonful Sugar.
1 Teaspoonful Green Mint.
The Juice of half a lemon.
The White of an Egg.
Cracek Ice.
Shake well and strain. Then serve.

GOLDEN FIZZ

2 Onzas Gin Gordon.
1 Cucharadita de azúcar.
½ Cucharadita de Curacao.
Jugo de ½ limón.
La yema de un huevo.
Hielo abundante. Muy batido y colado.

2 Ounces Gordon Gin.
1 Teaspoonful Sugar.
½ Teaspoonful Curacao.
The juice of ½ Lemon.
The York of 1 Egg.
Plenty of cracked ice.
Shake well and strain into glass.

GIN FIZZ

2 Onzas Gin Gordon.
1 Cucharadita azúcar.
Jugo de ½ limón.
Varias gotas Menta blanca.
Hielo menudo. Muy batido y después de colado agréguese un poco de agua de Seltz.

2 Ounces Gordon Gin.
1 Teaspoonful Sugar.
The Juice of ½ Lemon.
Several Dashes of white Creme de Menthe.
Crushed Ice.
Shake very well and strain; then add some Seltz water. Serve.

GOLDEN GLOVE
(Floridita Style)

2 Onzas Ron Jamaica.	2 Ounces Jamaica Rum.
1 Cucharadita Cointreau.	1 Teaspoonful Cointreau.
1 Cucharadita de azúcar.	1 Teaspoonful Sugar.
Jugo de ½ limón verde.	The Juice of ½ Lemon.
Hielo frappe. Batido eléctricamente. Sírvase frappe después de exprimirle encima una cáscara de naranja.	Cracked Ice. Shake in electrical shaker. Serve frapoe after squeezing in an orange peel.

GIN COCKTAIL

En un vaso de 10 onzas.	Use a 10-ounce glass.
Hielo menudo.	Cracked Ice.
Una ramita hierba buena.	1 Spring of Peppermint.
La cáscara de un limón verde con el jugo exprimido dentro.	1 Unripe Lemon Peei squeezing juice in glass.
½ Cucharadita de azúcar.	½ Teaspoonful Sugar.
1 Gota Angostura.	1 Dash Angostura.
½ Cucharadita Curacao.	½ Teaspoonful Curacao.
2 Onzas Gin Gordon.	2 Ounces Gordon Gin.
Agítese de un vaso para el otro. Sírvase colado.	Shake lightly and strain; then, serve.

GIN DAISSY

1 Copa llena de hielo menudo.	Take a glass and fill it with cracked ice; then put in:
½ Cáscara limón verde con jugo.	½ Unqueezed Lemon Peel.
1 Gota Angostura.	1 Dash Angostura.
½ Cucharadita de Chatreusse amarillo.	½ Teaspoonful Yellow Chartreuse.
2 Onzas Gin Gordon.	2 Ounces Gordon Gin.
½ Cucharadita de azúcar.	½ Teaspoonful Sugar.
4 Ramitas hierba buena.	4 Sprigs of Peppermint.
1 Guinda encima.	1 Cherry on top.
Sírvase sin colar.	Stir and serve without straining.

GOLDEN GATE

(Ideal para disipar en breves minutes los efectos del exceso alcohólico y poder continuar hasta lo infinito).
En un vaso de 10 onzas póngase hielo menudo y abundante.
El jugo de 2 limones.
Una cucharada de almíbar natural.
Una cucharada de bicarbonato.
Agua natural hasta llenarlo.
Bébase mientras está en efervecencia.

(Ideal pick me up to carry on a lengthy party).

In a glass of 10 oz. put plenty crushed ice.

The juice of ? lemons.

1 Spoonful of plain sirup.

1 Teaspoonful of bicarbonate.

Fill glass with spring water.

Drink while effervescent.

HAVANA BEACH

(Special)

½ Jugo piña.

½ Ron Martí.

1 Cucharadita azúcar.

Muy batido con hielo menudo. Sírvase colado.

½ Pineappie Juice.
½ Martí Rum.
1 Teaspoonful Sugar.
Cracked Ice.
Shake well and strain into cocktail glass.

HOT - KISS

½ Cognac Soberano.
½ Vermouth Martini Rossi
1 Cucharadita Curacao.
Enfríese sin batirlo y colado Sírvase con un par de guindas.

½ Soberano Cognac.
½ Martini Rossi Vermouth
1 Teaspoonful Curacao.
Do not shake. Strain and serve coul with two cherries.

IMPERIO ARGENTINA
(Special)

En una copita de dos Onz.
2 Partes de Crema de Cacao.
1 Parte de crema de leche fresca flotando.

In one small 2-ounce glass.
2 Parts Creme de Cacao.
1 Part fresh milk cream floating.

I D E A L

¼ Toronja.
1 Cucharadita Marraschino
1/3 Vermouth Martini Rossi
1/3 Vermouth Nolly Prat.
1/3 Gin Gordon.
Hielo menudo. Muy batido y colado. Sírvase con varias almendras.

¼ Grape Fruit.
1 Teaspoonful Marraschino
1/3 Martini Rossi Vermouth
1/3 Nolly Prat Vermouth.
1/3 Gordon Gin.
Cracked Ice.
Shake very well and strain into cocktail glass. Serve with a few almonds.

JOSEPHINE BAKER

½ Cognac Soberano.
½ Vino Ooorto.
1/3 Apricot Brandy.
1 Cucharadita de azúcar, la cáscara de un limón, la yema de un huevo.
Hielo menudito. Bien batido y colado. Canela por arriba.

½ Soberano Cognac.
½ Port Wine.
1/3 Apricot Brandy.
1 Teaspoonful Sugar.
1 Lemon Peel.
Yolk of an egg.
Cracked Ice.
Shake well and strain into cocktail glass. Cinnamon on top.

JABON CANDADO
(Ramoncito López special)

2 Onzas Ron "Martí".
1 Cucharadita de azúcar.
Jugo de ½ limón verde.
½ Clara de huevo.
Hielo menudo. Bien batido y colado.

2 Ounces "Martí" Rum.
1 Teaspoonful Sugar.
½ of the white of an egg.
Juice of half an unripe Lemon. Cracked Ice.
Shake well and strain into a cocktail glass.

LONGINES COCKTAIL

1/3 Cognac Soberano.
1/3 Anís del Mono.
1/3 Té fuerte
La piel de un limón.
1 Cucharadita de azúcar.
Hielo abundante, bien batido y colado.

1/3 Soberano Cognac.
1/3 Anís del Mono.
1/3 Strong Tea.
Peel of a lemon.
1 Teaspoonful of sugar.
Plenty ice, shake well and strain.

MANHATTAN
(Seco)

½ Vermouth Nolly Prat.
½ Rye Whiskey.
1 Gota Angostura.

Hielo menudo. Enfríese sin batirlo y cuélese

½ Nolly Prat Vermouth.
½ Rye Whiskey.
1 Dash Angostura.
Cracked Ice.

Do not shake. Let it become very cold, strain and serve.

MANHATTAN
(Dulce)

½ Vermouth Martini Rossi.
½ Rye Whiskey
½ Cucharadita de Curacao.

Hielo menudo Enfríese sin batirlo y cuélese. Sírvase con dos guindas.

½ Martini Rossi Vermouth.
½ Rye Whiskey.
½ Teaspoonful Curacao.
Cracked Ice.

Do not shake. Let it get very cold and strain.
Serve with two cherries.

MANHATTAN
(Medio Dulce)

½ Vermouth Nolly Prat.
½ Rye Whiskey.
1 Gota Angostura.

Hielo menudo. Enfríese sin batirlo y cuélese.

½ Nolly Prat Vermouth.
½ Rye Whiskey.
1 Dash Angostura.
Cracked Ice.

Do not shake. Let it become very cold, strain and serve.

MC AVOY

½ Vainilla ice cream.
½ Cognac Soberano.
Batido y colado.
Adórnese con canela en polvo..

½ Vainilla Ice-cream.
½ Soberano Cognac.

Shake and strain serve with powdered cinnamon on top.

MARTINI
(Seco)

½ Gin Gordon.
½ Vermouth Nolly Prat.
2 Gotas Orange Bitter.

Hielo menudo. Enfríese sin batirlo y cuélese. Sírvase con una aceituna.

½ Gordon Gin.
½ Nolly Prat Vermouth.
2 Dashes Orange Bitter.
Cracked Ice.

Do not Shake. Allow it to get very cold and strain. Serve with one olive.

MARTI-NI
(Demi-seco)

½ Gin Gordon.
½ Vermouth Nolly Prat.
2 Gotas Orange Bitter.

Hielo menudo. Enfríese sin batirlo y cuélese.

½ Gordon Gin.
½ Nolly Prat Vermouth.
2 Dashes Orange Biters.
Cracked Ice.
Do not Shake. Allow it to get very cold and strain. Then serve.

MARCO-ANTONIO

1/3 Jugo de toronja.
1 Cucharadita Marraschino.
2 Onzas Gin Gordon.
1 Cucharadita Granadina.
½ Clara huevo.
Hielo menudo. Batido y colado.

1/3 Grape Fruit Juice.
1 Teaspoonful Marrasquino.
2 Ounces Gordon Gin.
1 Teaspoonful Grenadine.
½ The white of an Egg.

Cracek Ice.
Shake well and strain into cocktail glass.

MARY PICKFORD

½ Jugo Piña.	½ Pineapple Juice.
½ Ron "Martí".	½ "Martí" Rum.
½ Cucharadita Granadina	½ Teaspoonful Grenadine.
	Crushed Ice.
Hielo menudo. Batido y colado.	Shake well and strain into cocktail glass.

MIAMI BEACH
(Special)

½ Jugo Piña.	½ Pineapple Juice.
½ Gin Gordon.	½ Gordon Gin.
1 Cucharadita de azúcar.	1 Teaspoonful Sugar.
	Cracked Ice
Hielo menudo. Batido y colado.	Shake well and strain into cocktail glass.

MIGUEL LIGERO
(Special)

2 Onzas Ron "Martí".	2 Ounces Rum "Martí".
1 Gota Angostura.	1 Drop Angostura.
½ Cucharadita Curazao.	½ Teaspoonful Curazao.
Jugo de ½ limón.	The juice of ½ lemon.
½ Cucharadita de azúcar.	½ Teaspoonful Sugar.
Bátase y cuélese.	Shake and strain.

MARY MORANDEYRA

1/3 Jugo Toronja.	1/3 Grape Fruit Juice.
1/3 Sloe Gin Gordon.	1/3 Gordon Sloe Gin.
1/3 Vermouth Martini Rossi	1/3 Martini Rossi Vermouth.
1 Cucharadita Marrasquino.	1 Teaspoonful Marraschino.
Hielo abundante menudo. Colado.	Plenty cracked ice, and strain it into a glass.

MENDIETA SPECIAL COCKTAIL

1/3 Vermouth italiano.
1/3 Vermouth Nolly Prat.
1/3 Old Tom Gin.
1/3 Cucharadita de Curacao.
Hielo menudo. Enfríese perfectamente y cuélese. Sírvase con dos guindas y corteza de naranja.

1/3 Italian Vermouth.
1/3 Nolly Prat Vermouth.
1/3 Old Tom Gin.
1/3 Teaspoonful of Curacao.
Crushed Ice.
Strain and serve ice with two cherries and peel of orange.

MENDEZ VIGO - SPECIAL

2 Onzas Cognac Tres Copas
1 Cucharadita azúcar.
1 Cucharadita Marraschino.
Jugo de ½ limón verde.
Hielo frappe. Batido eléctricamente. Sírvase frappe.

2 Oz. Tres Copas Cognas.
1 Teaspoonful Sugar.
1 Teaspoonful Marrasquino.
The Juise of ½ lemon.
Shake in electric shacker and serve frappe.

M E N T - J U L E P
(Mexican Style)

En un vaso de old fashion lleno de hielo menudo y con hierba buena abundante.
1 Cáscara de limón.
1 Cucharadita Marraschino
½ Vino Oporto.
½ Cognac Soberano.
1 Gota Angostura.
½ Cucharadita azúcar.
Agítese violentamente y sírvase con dos guindas y sin colar.

1 Old-fashioned glass full ice and plenty of peppermint.
1 Lemon Peel.
1 Teaspoonful Marrasquino
½ Port Wine.
½ Soberano Cognac.
1 Dash Angostura.
½ Teaspoonful Sugar.
Shake well. Serve with two cherries without straining.

MINT-JULEP
(Virginia Style)

Hierba buena abundante.
1 Cucharadita de azúcar.

Estrújese bien la hierba buena con el azúcar.

2 Onzas Rye Whiskey.
2 Gotas de limón.

Sírvase en un vaso lleno de hielo menudo y adornado con varias ramitas de hierba buena y una guinda.

Plenty of Peppermint leaves.
1 Teaspoonful Sugar.

Mix Peppermint leaves with Sugar.

2 Ounces Rye Whiskey.
2 Drops Lemon Juice.

Serve in a glass with plenty of cracked ice, and garnish with small sprigs of Mint and one cherry.

MISS JOAN KETCHUM SPECIAL COCKTAIL

½ Jugo de Piña.
½ Old Tom Gin.
1 Cucharadita de Apricot Brandy.
1 Cucharadita de Jarabe de Granadina.
Hielo menudo. Muy batido y colado.

½ Pineapple Juice.
½ Old Tom Gin.
1 Teaspoonful Apricot Brandy.
1 Teaspoonful Grenadine Sirup.
Crushed ice.
Shake well and strain.

MY-SIN COCKTAIL
(Manolo Solís Mendieta)

1 Onza Ajenjo.
1 Gota Angostura.
½ Clara de huevo.

Hielo abundante, bien batido y colado.

Humedézcase el borde del vaso con jugo de limón y azúcar en polvo.

1 Oz. Absinthe.
1 Oz. Anisette.
1 Drop Angostura.
½ White of an egg.

Plenty ice, shake well and strain.

Wet brim off glass with lemon juice and dust with powdered sugar

MOFUCO COCKTAIL

2 Onz. Ron "Martí".	2 Oz. "Martí" Run.
La corteza de un limón.	1 Peep of a lemon.
Una cucharadita de azúcar.	1 Teaspoonful of sugar.
Una gota de Angostura Bitters.	1 Drop Angostura Bitters.
Un huevo entero.	1 Whole egg.
Bátase perfectamente con hielo abundante y cuélese	Shake very well with plenty ice and strain.

MORNING STAR

½ Vino Oporto.	½ Port Wine.
½ Cognac Soberano.	½ Soberano Cognac.
1 Gota Angostura.	1 Dash Angostura.
1 Cucharadita de azúcar.	1 Teaspoonful Sugar.
1 Huevo entero.	1 Egg.
Hielo abundante.	Plenty Cracked Ice.
Muy batido. Sírvase colado y adornado con canela en polvo.	Shake well and strain into glass. Put some powdered cinnamon on top.

MONO COCKTAIL

2 Onzas Anís del Mono.	2 Ounces Anís del Mono.
2 Onzas Angostura.	1 Drop Angostura.
Hielo abundante, bien batido y colado.	Plenty ice. Shake well, strain and serve.

M O N J I T A

En una copa de 6 onzas.	Use a 10-ounce glass.
Hielo menudo	Cracked Ice
½ Agua carbonatada.	½ Sparkling water.
½ Anís del Mono (seco o dulce).	½ Anís del Mono (either dry or sweet).

MOJITO CRIOLLO

En un vaso de 8 onzas.
Hielo menudo. Varias ramitas hierba buena, la cáscara de un limón con el jugo exprimido dentro.
1 Cucharadita de azúcar.
2 Onzas Ron "Martí".
Agítese con la cuchara para que la hierba suelte el jugo. Agréguese agua carbonatada y sírvase sin colar.

Use an 8-ounce glass.
Cracked Ice.
Several sprigs of Mint.
1 Lemon Peel, squeezing juice into glass.
1 Teaspoonful Sugar.
2 Ounces "Martí" Rum.
Stil with spoon.
Add sparkling water and serve without straining.

MOJITO CRIOLLO NUM. 2

En un vaso de 8 onzas.
Hielo menudo.
Varias ramitas hierba buena.
La cáscara de un limón con el jugo exprimido dentro.
1 Cucharadita de azúcar.
2 Onzas Ginebra Gordon.
Agítese con la cuchara para que la hierba suelte el jugo. Agréguese agua carbonatada y sírvase sin colar.

Use an 8-ounce glass.
Cracked Ice.
Several sprigs of Mint.
1 Lemon Peel, squeezing juice into glass.
1 Teaspoonful Sugar.
2 Ounces Gordon's Gin.
Stil with spoon.
Add sparkling water and serve without straining.

MURIEL ESPECIAL

2 Onzas Ron "Martí" Carta Oro.
1 Cucharada de azúcar.
1 Cucharadita Jugo de Toronja.
1 Cucharadita Marraschino.
Jugo ½ limón verde.
Hielo frappe.
Batido y sírvase frappe.

2 Ounces Ron "Martí" Gold Label
1 Tablespoonful Sugar.
1 Teaspoonful Grape Fruit Juice.
1 Teaspoonful Marrasquino.
The juice of ½ lemon.
Frappe Ice.
Shake well and serve frappe.

MOJITO CRIOLLO Nº 3

En un vaso de 8 onzas.
Hielo menudo.
Varias ramitas hierba buena.
La cáscara de un limón verde con el jugo exprimido dentro del vaso.
2 Onzas Cogñac Soberano.
1 Cucharadita de azúcar.
Agítese con la cuchara para que la hierba suelte el jugo.
Agréguese agua carbonatada y sirva sin colar.

Use an 8 ounce glass.
Cracked Ice.
Several sprigs of mint.
1 Lemon Peel, squeezing juice into glass.
2 Ounces Soberano Cognac.
1 Teaspoonful Sugar.
Stir with spoon.
Add sparkling water and serve without straining.

MARTI FLIP

1 Copa Ron Martí.
1 Cucharadita de azúcar.
1 Huevo entero.
Hielo menudo.
Muy batido y sírvase colado y adornado con canela en polvo.

1 Glass Martí Rum.
1 Spoonful Sugar.
1 Egg.
Plenty Cracked Ice.
Shake well and strain; then, serve with powdered cinnamon on top.

NATIONAL COCKTAIL

1/4 Apricot Brandy.
1/4 Jugo piña.
1/2 Ron "Martí".
Hielo menudo.
Batido y colado.
Adórnese con lascas de piña y guindas.

1/4 Apricot Brandy.
1/4 Pineapple Juice.
1/2 "Martí" Rum.
Cracked Ice.
Shake well and strain in cocktail glass.
Garnish glass with slices of pineapple and cherries.

ORANGE BLOSSOM

½ Jugo naranja.
½ Gin Gordon.
½ Cucharada Granadina.
Hielo menudo. Batido y colado.

½ Orange Juice.
½ Gordon Gin.
½ Spoonful Grenadine.
Cracked Ice.
Shake well and strain into a cocktail glass.

OJEN COCKTAIL

2 Onzas Ojén.
2 Gotas Angostura.
Hielo abundante. Batido y colado.

2 Ounces Ojen
2 Dashes Angostura.
Plenty of Cracked ice.
Shake well and strain; then serve.

OLD FASHION WHISKEY

En un vaso de old fashion lleno de hielo.
Varias ramitas hierba buena
1 Cáscara entera de limón exprimiéndolo adentro.
½ Cucharadita azúcar.
½ Cucharadita Curacao.
2 Onzas Rye Whiskey.
Agítese violentamente y sírvase sin colarlo adornado con lascas de piña, naranja y guindas.

1 Old Fashion glass full of cracked ice. Several mint leaves.
1 Comolete Lemon Peel, squeezed into glass.
½ Teaspoonful Sugar.
½ Teaspoonful Curacao.
2 Ounces Rye Whiskey.
Shake well. Do not strain. Serve in glass garnished with slices of pineapple, orange and cherries.

OLD SMUGGLER'S AWAKEN

2 Onzas Ginebra Bols.
1 Cucharada de azúcar.
1 Gota Angostura.
1 Huevo entero.
La piel de un limón verde
Hielo menudo. Batido y colado.
Adórnese con canela en polvo.

2 Ounces Bols Gin.
1 Spoonful Sugar.
1 Dash Angostura.
1 Egg.
The peel of an unripe lemon
Cracked Ice.
Shake well and strain into cocktail glass.
Powdered cinnamon on top.

PARIS MIDI

En una copa de 10 onzas.
Hielo menudo.
1/3 Crema Cassis.
2/3 Vermouth Nolly Prat.
Agua carbonatada.
Agítese con una cucharita y sírvase.

Use a 10-ounce glass.
Cracked Ice.
1/3 Creme Cassis.
2/3 Nolly Prat Vermouth.
Sparkling water.
Stir with a spoon and serve.

PALM OLIVE
(Cocktail Especial)

½ Jugo de toronja.
½ Ginebra Gordon's.
1 Cucharadita menta verde
Hielo menudo, abundante y bien batido y colado, sírvase en un vaso de 6 onzas.

½ Juice of a Grape Fruit.
½ Gordon's Gin.
½ Teaspoonful green mint.
Plenty of ice shake well and strain serve in a 6 ounce-glass.

PABLO ALVAREZ DE CAÑAS
(Special)

1 onza de Jerez "Tio Pepe".
1 onza Coñac "Tres Copas".
1 cucharadita Crema de Cacao.
1 cucharadita Brandy de Cereza.
½ Cucharadita de azúcar.
Corteza de ¼ de limón.
Bátase con bastante hielo y sírvase sin colar, adornado con lascas de piña y naranjas y dos cerezas.

1 ounce Sherry "Tio Pepe".
1 ounce "Tres Copas" cognac.
1 small spoon Creme Cacao.
1 small spoon Cherry Brand.
½ small spoon sugar.
Cap peel of one lemon.
Shake with plenty of ice and serve it without straining, adorned with slices of pineapple and orange and 2 cherries.

PEPIN RIVERO
(Special)

1/3 Leche fresca.
1/3 Crema Cacao.
1/3 Gin Gordon.
1/6 Cointreau.
½ Cucharadita de azúcar.
Hielo abundante. Muy batido y colado.

1/3 Sweet Milk.
1/3 Creme de Cacao.
1/3 Gordon Gin.
1/6 Cointreau.
½ Teaspoonful Sugar.
Plenty of Ice.
Shake well and strain; then serve.

PERLITA GRECO
(Special)

½ Dubonnet.
½ Cognac Soberano.
½ Cucharadita de Curacao.
Enfríese y cuélese sin batirlo.

½ Dubonnet.
½ Soberano Cognac.
½ Teaspoonful Curacao.
Do not shake. Strain and serve very cold.

PEGGY NILES
(Special)

2 Oz. Ron "Martí" Oro.
½ Jugo de un limón.
½ Cucharadita de azúcar.
1 Cucharadita Elíxir "Martí".
Batido eléctricamente con hielo frappe, sírvase en una copa de cocktail.

2 Ounces "Martí" Rum. (Gold).
Juice of a half lemon.
½ Teaspoonful Sugar.
1 Teaspoonful of Elíxir "Martí".
Shake in a electric shaker with crushed ice.
Serve in a cocktail glass.

"PRECIOS FIJOS" - MANOLITO SANCHEZ
(Special)

2 Oz. Sloe Gin.
1 Cucharadita de jugo de naranja.
1 Cucharadita de Apricot Brandy.
½ Cucharadita de jarabe Granadina.
Hielo abundante. En una copa de forma cónica de 6 onzas, adornado con lascas de piña y 2 guindas.

2 oz. Sloe Gin
1 Teaspoonful of orange juice.
1 Teaspoonful of Apricot Brandy.
½ Teaspoonful Granadine Sirup.
Plenty ice. In a conic glass of 6 oz. Serve with slices of pineapple and 2 cherries.

PRESIDENTE COCKTAIL

½ Vermouth Chambery.
½ Ron "Marti" (Oro).
½ Cucharadita de Curacao.
Hielo menudo.
Enfríese perfectamente y cuélese.
Sírvase con guindas y una corteza de naranja.

½ Chambery Vermouth.
½ "Marti" Rum (Gold Label).
½ Teaspoonful of Curacao.
Crushed ice.
Cool well and strain.
Serve with cherries and a peel of orange.

PISCO PUNCH

Jugo de 1 limon.
Una gota Angostura.
½ Cucharadita de azúcar.
2 Onzas Aguardiente de Usa, bien batido y colado.
Sírvase en una copa impregnada de anisette con dos guindas.

Juice of 1 lemon.
Dash Angostura.
½ Teaspoonful Sugar.
2 Ounces Grape brandy.
Cracked ice shake well and strain serve in a glass with anisette and two cherries.

PRESIDENTE MENOCAL SPECIAL

En un vaso de 8 onzas póngase hierba buena abundante.
Una cucharadita de azúcar.
Varias gotas de limón.
Estrújese bien la hierba buena.
2 Onzas de Ron "Martí".
Llénese el vaso de hielo menudo y adórnese con un ramito de hierba buena entero y dos guindas.

In a glass of 8 ounces put plenty of Mint leaves.

1 Teaspoonful of sugar.

Several drops of Lemon juice and crushed mint leaves.

2 Oz. "Martí" Rum.

Fill glass with crushed ice; serve with Pepper-mint and two cherries.

P. ARANGO

½ Vermouth Nolly Prat.
½ Ron "Martí, Carta Oro.
Enfríese y cuélese "no batido". Sírvase con una cáscara de naranja en copa alta.

½ Nolly Prat Vermouth.
½ "Martí" Rum (Gold).
Cool and strain "do not shake". Serve with a orange peel a cocktail glass.

PICK - ME - UP

½ Dubonnet.
½ Cognac Soberano.
1/3 Anisette.
1 Cáscara de limón.
½ Clara de huevo.

Hielo menudo. Batido y colado.

½ Dubonnet.
½ Soberano Cognac.
1/3 Anisette.
1 Lemon Peel.
½ The white of an Egg.
Cracked Ice.
Shake well and strain into a cocktail glass.

PORTO FLIP

1 Copa Vino Oporto.	1 Glass Port Wine.
1 Cucharada de azúcar.	1 Spoonful Sugar.
1 Huevo entero.	1 Whole Egg.
Hielo abundante.	Plenty cracked ice.
Muy batido y sírvase colado y adornado con canela en polvo.	Shake well and strain; then, serve with powdered cinnamon on top.

POUSSE CAFE

½ Cognac Tres Copas.	½ Tres Copas Cognac.
1/3 Anisette.	1/3 Anisette.
1/3 Crema Cacao.	1/3 Creme de Cacao.
1 Cucharadita de Café puro.	1 Teaspoonful Black Coffee.
Enfríese y sírvase sin hielo.	Serve cold without ice.

COCKTAIL GLORIA

(Dedicado a Gloria de la C. M.)

3/3 Ginebra Gordon's.	3/3 Gordon's Gin.
1/3 Vino Dubonnet.	1/3 Dubonnet Wine.
2 Gotas Ajenjo.	2 Dashes of Ajenjo.
Enfríese con hielo abundante; sírvase en copa de cocktail.	Cool well with plenty of ice serve in a cocktail glass.

PLANTERS - PUNCH

Una copa de las usadas para el champagne. Llena de hielo.

El jugo de ½ limón.

1 Cucharadita de Curacao.

1 Cucharadita Granadina.

2 Onzas Ron Jamaica.

Sírvase sin colar, adornado de lascas de piña, naranja y limón.

Take a glass and fill it with cracked ice. Then put in:

The Juice of ½ Lemon.

1 Teaspoonful Curacao.

1 Teaspoonful Grenadine.

2 Ounces Jamaica Rum.

Serve without straining in glass garnished with slices of pineapple, orange and Lemon.

RAUL NAVARRETE
(Special)

1/3 Crema fresca leche.

1/3 Coñac "Tres Copas".

1/3 Crema Cacao.

1 Cucharadita de azúcar.

La piel entera de un limón. Hielo menudo. Muy batido y colado.

1/3 Fresh Sweet Cream.

1/3 "Tres Copas" Cognac.

1/3 Creme de Cacao.

1 Teaspoonful Sugar.

1 Full Lemon Peel.

Plenty of cracked ice. Shake well and strain into cocktail glass.

RAMOS GIN FIZZ
(Special)

2 Onzas Gin Gordon.

El jugo de ½ limón.

1 Cucharadita jarabe almendras.

1 Cucharadita agua de azahar.

½ Onza crema fresca.

Bien batido y colado.

2 Ounces Gordon Gin.

The Juice of ½ Lemon.

1 Teaspoonful Almond Sirup

1 Teaspoonful Orange-flower Water.

½ Ounce Fresh Cream.

Shake well and strain in cocktail glass.

— **De "TRES COPAS" una copa, antes de tomar la sopa** —

"REX"
(Special)

En una copa de 10 onzas.	Use a 10-ounce glass.
Hielo menudo.	Cracked Ice.
La piel de un limòn francés.	The peel of a French lemon.
¼ Bitter Solamer.	¼ Bitters.
¾ Vermouth Martini Rossi.	¾ Martini Rossi Vermouth.
Agua carbonatada.	Sparkling Water.
Sírvase sin colar.	Serve without straining.

RUBI SILVER COCKTAIL

½ Sloe Gin Gordon.	½ Gordon Gin Sloe.
½ Cherry Brandy.	½ Cherry Brandy.
El jugo de un limón.	1 Lemon Juice.
½ Clara de huevo.	½ White of an Egg.
Hielo abundante muy batido y colado.	Plenty ice. Shake very well and strain.

RAINBOW
(After dinner drink)

Insuperable.	Insuperable.
Chartreuse.	Chartreuse.
Curacao.	Curacao.
Marraschino.	Marrasquino.
Parfait Amour.	Parfait Amour.
Peppermint.	Pepper-mint.
Cacao.	Cacao.
Póngase muy despacio en una copa alta, empezando por el último o sea el Cacao.	Pour very slowly into a long glass, starting with the last, namely, the cacao.

RUM COCKTAIL

En un vaso de 10 onzas.
Hielo menudo.
Una ramita hierba buena.
La cáscara de un limón.
verde con el jugo exprimido dentro.
½ Cucharadita de azúcar.
1 Gota Angostura.
½ Cucharadita de Curacao.
2 Onzas Ron "Martí".
Agítese de un vaso para el otro. Sírvase colado.

Use a 10-ounce glass.
Cracked Ice.
1 Unripe Lemon Peel, Squeezing juice in glass.
½ Teaspoonful Sugar.
1 Dash Angostura.
½ Teaspoonful Curacao.
2 Ounces "Martí" Rum.
Shake lightly and strain; then, serve.

ROYAL FIZZ

2 Onzas Gin Gordon.
1 Cucharadita de azúcar.
½ Cucharadita de Curacao.
Jugo de ½ limón verde.
1 Huevo completo.
Hielo menudo. Muy batido y colado.

2 Ounces Gordon Gin.
1 Teaspoonful Sugar.
½ Teaspoonful Curacao.
The Juice of ½ Unripe Lemon.
1 Whole egg (the white and the yolk).
Cracked Ice.
Shake well and strain. Then serve.

ROSE

1/3 Gin Gordon.
1/3 Calvados Apple Jack.
1/3 Vermouth Nolly Prat.
½ Cucharadita Granadina.
1 Cáscara de limón.
Hielo menudo. Batido y colado. Sírvase con guindas.

1/3 Gordon Gin.
1/3 Calvados Apple Jack.
1/3 Nolly Prat Vermouth.
½ Teaspoonful Grenadine.
The peel of a Lemon.
Plenty Cracked Ice.
Shake well and strain into cocktail glass with cherries.

RUM DAISSY

Una copa llena de hielo menudo.
1 Gota Angostura.
½ Cucharadita de Chartreuse amarillo.
2 Onzas Ron "Martí".
½ Cáscara limón con jugo.
½ Cucharadita azúcar.
Unas ramitas hierba buena.
Dos guindas y frutas estación. Sírvase sin colar.

1 Glass full of cracked ice.
1 Dash Angostura.
½ Teaspoonful Yellow Chartreuse.
2 Ounces "Martí" Rum.
½ Unsqueezed Lemon Peel.
½ Teaspoonful Sugar.
Several sprigs of mint.
Two cherries and season fruits. Stir and serve without straining.

SMALL - DINGER

½ Gordon Gin.
¼ Ron Martí.
¼ Granadina.
¼ Jugo Limón.
Hielo frappé abundante. Bátese ligeramente y cuélese.

½ Gordon Gin.
½ Martí Rum.
¼ Grenadine.
¼ Lemon Juice.
Frappé Ice.
Shake and strain.

SUMMER WELLES SPECIAL

½ Vermouth Italiano.
½ Whiskey C. Club.
1 Cucharadita de Amer Picón.
½ Cucharadita de Curacao.
1 Gota de Angostura Bitters.
½ Cucharadita de azúcar. Hielo menudo, batido y colado.
Sírvase con una ramita de hierba buena y dos guindas verdes.

½ Italian Vermouth.
½ C. Club Whiskey.
1 Teaspoonful Amer Picón
½ Teaspoonful Curacao.
1 Drop Angostura Bitters.
½ Teaspoonful of sugar Crushed ice.
Shake and strain.
Serve with mint leaves and two green cherries.

SNOW BALL

1/3 Gin Gordon.
1/3 Parfait Amour.
1/3Crema Menta verde.
1/3 Leche fresca.

Hielo menudo. Muy batido y colado.

1/3 Gordon Gin.
1/3 Parfait Amour.
1/3 Green Creme de Menthe.
1/3 Fresh milk.
Cracked Ice.
Shake well and strain into cocktail glass.

SHERRY COBBLER
(Special)

1 onza de Jerez "Tío Pepe".
1 onza Coñac "Tres Copas".
1 cucharadita Crema de Cacao.
1 cucharadita Brandy de Cereza.
½ Cucharadita de azúcar.
Corteza de ¼ de limón.
Bátase con bastante hielo y sírvase sin colar, adornado con lascas de piña y naranjas y dos cerezas.

1 ounce "Tio Pepe" Sherry.
1 ounce "Tres Copas" Cognac.
1 small spoon Creme Cacao.
1 small spoon Cherry Brand.
½ small spoon sugar.
Cap peel of one lemon.
Shake with plenty of ice and serve it without straining, adorned with slices of pineapple and orange and 2 cherries.

SUISSE

½ Absinthe Pernot.
½ Agua natural.
¼ Anisette o bien jarabe natural.
½ Clara de huevo.
Hielo menudo.
Batido y sírvase colado.

½ Pernot Absinthe.
½ Natural Water.
¼ Anisette or Plain Syrup.
½ White of an eeg.
Cracked Ice.
Shake well and strain; then serve.

SHERRY FLIP

1 Copa Jerez Seco La Ina.
1 Cucharadita azúcar.
1 Huevo completo.
Hielo abundante.
Muy batido y sírvase colado y adornado con canela en polvo.

1 Glass Dry Sherry Wine.
1 Teaspoonful Sugar.
1 Egg.
Plenty cracked ice.
Shake well and strain into cocktail glass.
Serve with powdered cinnamon on top.

SAN MARTIN

1/3 Ginebra Old Tom.
1/3 Vermouth Nolly Prat.
1/3 Vermouth Martini Rossi.
1 Cucharadita de Anisette.
1 Gota de Angostura.
Hielo menudito.
Muévase con una cuchara y cuélese. Al borde de la copa humedézcase con limón y azúcar.

1/3 Old Tom Gin.
1/3 Nolly Prat Vermouth.
1/3 Martini Rossi Vermouth.
1 Teaspoonful Anisette.
1 Drop Angostura.
Plenty of cracked ice. Stir with a spoon. Strain and serve in cocktail glass. Wet brim of glass with lemon and sugar.

SEVILLANA

1 Gota Angostura.
½ Cucharadita Curacao.
½ Cucharadita azúcar.
½ Vermouth Martini Rossi.
½ Ginebra Bols.
Varias ramitas hierba buena con su jugo.
Agítese de un vaso para otro. Sírvase colado y con un par de guindas.

1 Dash Angostura.
½ Teaspoonful Curacao.
½ Teaspoonful Sugar.
½ Martini Rossi Vermouth.
½ Bols Gin.
1 Lemon Peel unsqueezed.
Stir and strain; then, serve with a couple of cherries.

S. O. S. COCKTAIL

1/2 Cucharadita Raspail.
1/3 Vermouth Nolly Prat.
1/2 Vermouth Martini Rossi
1/3 Old Tom Gin.
Hielo menudo.
Agítese sin batirlo y sírvase colado con lascas de piña longitudinales y varias guindas.

1/2 Teaspoonful Raspail.
1/3 Nolly Prat Vermouth.
1/2 Martini Rossi Vermouth
1/3 Old Tom Gin.
Cracked Ice.
Stir and strain; then, serve with slices of pineapple and several cherries.

SLOE GIN FIZZ

2 Onzas Sloe Gin Gordon.
½ Cucharadita Curacao.
½ Cucharadita Amer Picón
½ Cucharadita azúcar.
Jugo de ½ limón verde.

Hielo abundante. Batido y colado.

2 Ounces Gordon's Sloe Gin.
½ Teaspoonful Curacao.
½ Teaspoonful Amer Picon
½ Teaspoonful Sugar.
The Juice of ½ Unripe Lemon Plenty of ice.
Shake well and strain in cocktail glass.

STINGER
(After dinner drink)

½ Cognac Soberano.
½ Menta blanca.
Hielo menudo. Bien batido y colado.

½ Soberano Cognac.

½ White Creme de Menthe.

Cracked Ice.

Shake well and strain in cocktail glass.

SILVER FIZZ

2 Onzas Gin Gordon.	2 Ounces Gordon Gin.
1 Cucharadita azúcar.	1 Teaspoonful Sugar.
1 Clara de huevo.	The White of 1 Egg.
Jugo de ½ limón.	Several Dashes of white Creme de Menthe.
Varias gotas menta blanca.	Shake well and strain into glass.
Muy batido y colado.	

SOBERANO BRANDY HIGHBALL

Vasito de Cognac Soberano.	Small glass of Soberano Cognac.
Pedazo de hielo.	Plenty Cracked Ice.
¼ agua mineral aparte.	¼ of mineral water.

SEVENTH HEAVEN

La piel de un limón sin jugo.	1 Lemon Peel Squeezed.
½ Cucharadita Fernet Branca.	½ Teaspoonful Fernet-Branca.
½ Vermouth Martini Rossi	½ Martini Rossi Vermouth
½ Sloe Gin Gordon.	½ Gordon's Sloe Gin.
¼ Cucharadita azúcar.	¼ Teaspoonful Sugar.
Hielo. Batido y colado.	Cracked Ice.
Sirvase con varias almendras o nueces.	Shake well and strain into cocktail glass. Serve with several almonds or walnuts.

SMOKED COCKTAIL

½ Cucharadita Curacao.	½ Teaspoonful Curacao.
1 Cucharadita de azúcar	1 Teaspoonful Sugar.
2 Onzas Scoth Whiskey.	2 Ounces Scoth Whiskey.
Hierba buena.	Mint Leaf.
½ Limón con su jugo y cáscara.	½ Lemon and peel.
Hielo menudo.	Cracked Ice.
Agítese de un vaso para el otro y sirvase colado.	Shake well from one glass to another, strain and serve.

SMOKED COCKTAIL

Benjamín Menéndez
(Special)

½ Cucharadita Curacao.
1 Cucharadita azúcar.
2 Onzas Scoth Whiskey.
Hierba buena.
½ Limón con su jugo y cáscara.
Hielo menudo.
Agítese de un vaso para el otro y sírvase colado.

½ Teaspoonful Curacao.
1 Teaspoonful Sugar.
2 Ounces Scoth Whiskey.
1 Sprig of Mint.
½ Lemon (Juice and peel)
Cracked Ice.
Shake lightly and strain; then serve.

TEQUILA COCKTAIL

Una vaso de 20 onzas de Tequila puro.
El jugo de un limón.
Una cucharadita de azúcar.
Una gota de Angostura.
Hielo abundante, bien batido y colado.

In a 20 onunce glass of Pure Tequila.
A lemon juice.
1 Teaspoonful of Sugar.
1 Drop Angostura.
Plenty of ice, shake well and strain.

VERSAILLES CLUB

½ Dubonnet.
½ Cognac Soberano.
½ Cucharadita de Curacao.
Enfríese y cuélese sin batirlo.

½ Dubonnet.
½ Soberano Cognac.
½ Teaspoonful Curacao.
Do not shake. Strain and serve very cold.

VERMOUTH
(American Style)

2 Onzas Martini Rossi.
2 Cucharaditas Amer Picon.
½ Cucharadita Curacao.
1 Gota de Angostura.
1 Cáscara de limõn.
1 Ramita hierba buena.
½ Cucharadita de azúcar.
Hielo menudo. Batido y colado. Sírvase con un par de guindas.

2 Ounces Martini Rossi.
1 Teaspoonful Amer Picon.
½ Teaspoonful Curacao.
1 Dash Angostura.
1 Lemon Peel.
1 Small Sprig of Mint.
½ Teaspoonful Sugar.
Cracked Ice.
Shake well and strain into cocktail glass. Serve with a couple of cherries.

VERMOUTH
(Colonial Style)

Un vaso old fashion lleno de hielo menudo.
½ Cucharadita de azúcar.
1 Cáscara de limón exprimido dentro del vaso.
1 Gota de Angostura.
1 Ramita hierba buena.
½ Cucharadita Curacao.
1 Cucharadita Amer Picon
2 Onzas Vermouth Martini Rossi para llenar el vaso.
Agítese violentamente y sírvase con un colador adecuado.

1 Old Fashioned Glass of crushed ice.
½ Teaspoonful Sugar.
1 Lemon Peel Squeezed into the glass.
1 Dash Angostura.
1 Small Sprig of Mint.
½ Teaspoonful Curacao.
1 Teaspoonful Amer Picon
2 Ounces Martini Rossi Vermouth to fill glass.
Shake well and strain, then serve.

VELVET PUNCH

½ Guinness Stout Beer.
½ Champagne.
Todo frío y servido al natural.

½ Guinnes Stout Beer.
½ Champagne.
Serve cold, but without cracked ice

ZAZERAC

2 Onzas Rye Whiskey.
1 Cucharadita Anisette.
2 Gotas Argostura.
La piel completa de un limón verde.
Hielo menudo. Batido y colado.

El borde de la copa impregnado de limón y azúcar. Con la piel del limón dentro en espiral.

2 Ounces Rye Whiskey.
1 Teaspoonful Anisette.
2 Dashes Angostura.
1 Lemon Peel.
Cracked Ice.

Shake well and strain. Frost brim of glass with sugar and lemon. Juice leaving peel inside glass.

VERMOUTH
(Rafaelito M. - Special)

Un vaso old fashion lleno de hielo menudo.
½ Cucharadita de azúcar.
1 Cáscara de limón exprimido dentro del vaso.
1 Gota de Angostura.
1 Ramita hierba buena.
½ Cucharadita de Curacao
1 Cucharadita Amer Picón
2 Onzas Vermouth Martini Rossi para llenar el vaso.
1 Onza Rey Whiskey.
Agítese violentamente y sírvase con un colador adecuado.

1 Old Fashioned Glass of crushed ice.
½ Teaspoonful Sugar.
1 Lemon Peel Squeezed into the glass.
1 Dash Angostura.
1 Spring Pepper-mint.
½ Teaspoonful Curacao.
1 Teaspoonful Amer Picon
2 Ounces Martini Rossi Vermouth to fill glass.
1 Ounce Rey Whiskey.
Shake well and strain, then serve.

CPSIA information can be obtained
at www.ICGtesting.com
Printed in the USA
LVHW030937150521
687527LV00005B/290